FORGOTTEN VOICES

Malcolm McKay

FORGOTTEN VOICES

Adapted from *Forgotten Voices of The Great War*
by Max Arthur

OBERON BOOKS
LONDON

WWW.OBERONBOOKS.COM

First published in this adaptation in 2007 by Oberon Books Ltd
521 Caledonian Road, London N7 9RH
Tel: 020 7607 3637 / Fax: 020 7607 3629
e-mail: info@oberonbooks.com
www.oberonbooks.com

Forgotten Voices of The Great War first published in 2003
by Ebury Press.

Cover design by snowcreative

ISBN: 9781840027891

Characters

NEWTON
KITTY
HARRIS
TODD
HAINES

Forgotten Voices was first performed on 1 June 2007 at the Riverside Studios, London. Cast and crew were as follows:

Captain Peter Newton	**Rupert Frazer**
Kitty Proctor	**Belinda Lang**
Private Kidder Harris	**Matthew Kelly**
Sergeant Lawrence Todd	**Timothy Woodward**
Private Joe Haines	**Steven Crossley**
Directed and adapted by	**Malcolm McKay**
Designer	**Douglas Heap**
Lighting Designer	**Gerry Jenkinson**
Costumes	**Maya Degerlund**
Assistant Director	**Sophy Westendarp**
Company Stage Manager (London)	**Natalie Brook-Reynolds**
	Roger Bruce (Edinburgh)
Production Manager	**Barbra Egervary**
Set painters	**Anna Stamper** & **Belinda Clisham**
PR	**Peter Leone** & **Ian Stirling** (Arthur Leone PR)
Graphic design	**snowcreative** www.snowcreative.co.uk
Marketing consultants	**Target-Live.com**
Producer	**Louise Chantal**
Production Associate	**Maria Kempinska**
Executive Producer	**William Burdett-Coutts**

The play is set in the gallery of the Imperial War Museum in the late 1950s, and is based on real oral testimonies of the Great War as recorded for the Sound Archive of the museum.

THE IMPERIAL WAR MUSEUM

The art gallery of the museum, a beautiful space. On the walls some of the great paintings of World War One. Maybe the huge 'Gassed', by John Singer Sargent.

Wooden banquettes in front of the paintings.

The time is the late 1950s.

(Note: All characters are middle-aged. They have come to the Imperial War Museum to relate their experiences of the First World War. They hear and acknowledge each other as they tell their stories; are sometimes inspired by these, and sometimes involved in their own thoughts and memories. It's important to remember that this is often the first time they have told many of these stories and it can be quite an emotional release to be able to speak out their past to others who were there and will understand.)

PETER NEWTON, a solemn, public school educated, ex-army captain, sits to one side. He's a nervy man. He writes obsessively in a large and battered notebook.

KITTY PROCTOR comes in. She's a tough attractive woman from the North of England. She's been hit hard in her life, but faces it with a brave, if sentimental, humour and doggedness. She carries a cup of tea. She looks around at the gallery and then at NEWTON.

KITTY: You done?

NEWTON may nod, but doesn't look up from his notebook.

Didn't think there'd be so many of us.

She smiles.

All them tape recorders and notebooks. I didn't think we were so important, did you? It's the whole thing, they said, they want all of it recorded for posterity. All our memories.

A brief pause.

I'm the only woman today, you know? They said we want the civilian point of view as well; the home front, as it were. I'm Kitty Proctor by the way, well I were Walker then.

NEWTON: Good morning.

NEWTON continues to write. KITTY sits down.

KITTY: I was ring spinner in mill. I was when it started anyhow. I just told them. We worked six days a week from six in the morning till half past five at night and I got the large sum of fifteen and six a week for it. Better than that now in't it? At least you can say that. Except for the music. You heard them Beatles? I quite like it really. Always liked music. Then too. Did you?

NEWTON: Ah?

KITTY: Don't you know?

Smile.

Sorry. I'm talking too much.

NEWTON: Yes I did. I like music. Very much.

KITTY: It's all that, with them taking it down, brings it all up, doesn't it?

NEWTON: (*Thoughtful.*) I liked it then, certainly.

KITTY: Me too. There were a lot of music then. All the mills had their own bands you know. The music's what started it. Did for me anyway. Well. No. That's not true.

Little pause.

It started with him of course.

NEWTON: Him?

KITTY: My husband.

She stops as if she wants to go on.

It doesn't matter.

NEWTON: (*Gently.*) Your husband?

KITTY: (*A little tearful.*) It's the same old feelings isn't it? Never go, do they? And once they start you can't stop them. Don't know whether I told them everything. Just bare bones really, but not everything.

A pause.

It's him, I should have told about. How I met him, and...so on. I had a nice friend, you see?

NEWTON: Yes.

KITTY: Well. Me, and my friend, we used to go out dancing at night. Nothing to it really. And we met these two young fellahs...

She smiles as she remembers. He smiles with her.

...and I liked mine very much and he liked me, you see, and we started courting and I found out he was only in lodgings and didn't have no father and no mother. He was a lovely man. Finally we made our minds up to get married, and we saved our money and got a house in Shipley for three and six a week. Not much now, is it? We were happy, very happy. He would go to his work and I would go to the mill. He thought the world of me and I thought the world of him. At nights when he used to be at home, I had lovely hair in those days, and he used to do my hair up for me, in all kinds of styles.

Stops.

And then it came to be that the war started. And before we knew where we were it were all round us, wasn't it?

She turns as KIDDER HARRIS comes in. He was a private in the war. He's a bit of a charmer, with a vibrant, attractive personality, who often sings or whistles to himself. He holds a pint of bitter and half sings/hums a snatch of 'Swanee'. He looks up the painting.

HARRIS sings the first two lines of 'Swanee'. Drinks.

HARRIS: Look what they gave me, pint an' all, didn't expect that.

Hand out.

Harris. Kidder Harris. Private. As was. East Lancs.

NEWTON: Newton. Peter Newton.

As if reluctant.

Captain.

HARRIS: You must have got a bloody tape recorder then.

Just pen and note pad, me.

To KITTY.

Hullo love.

KITTY: Hullo.

HARRIS: Come all the way down here on night train, just to talk about it. I didn't think how much was there, all bottled up.

He takes an attendant's chair and sets it down to look at the paintings properly.

KITTY: I was just saying.

NEWTON: Yes, we were. We were talking.

(*To KITTY.*) I was in Gibraltar when it started, and was afraid it would be over too quickly and I should miss it. That's what I felt then, afraid I would miss it.

HARRIS: (*Looking at painting.*) We were all the same.

KITTY: Don't I know it?

NEWTON: We were such keen soldiers, you know, and if there was a war in which the British Army was taking part we were, well I was, only too anxious to be at the Front.

He's essentially talking to KITTY, but HARRIS, being the garrulous sort, joins in.

HARRIS: Don't know about the front, didn't think about that, but joining up, that was another matter. I quite agree.

KITTY: Well us, we had a friend who'd enlisted in Canada. And this is where the music comes in. He asked us would we go to the Alhambra? We didn't know what was on, but thought it would be a great treat...

HARRIS: Aye it would. I can remember the Alhambra. Used to be everywhere weren't they?

KITTY: ...so we said, 'Aye, we would!' When we got there everything was lovely. Vesta Tilley was on stage, dressed in a beautiful gown of either silver or gold, but what we didn't know until we arrived was that also on stage amongst the greenery were army officers with tables all set out for recruiting. Vesta introduced those songs, you know, 'We Don't Want To Lose You, But We Think You Ought To Go.'

HARRIS whistles a bit of 'Rule Britannia'. She smiles.

And that, that's it, Rule Britannia, and all those kind of things. Then she come off the stage and walked round the audience – up and down, either sides, down middle – and the young men were getting up and following her, and when she got to our row she hesitated a bit. I couldn't bear it, I wanted her to go away. I don't quite know what happened but she put her hand on my husband's shoulder, he was on the end seat, and as the men were all following her, he got up and followed her too.

(*Getting upset.*) They all went on the stage, their names were taken and they received the king's shilling right there and then. That meant they were recruited for the army. When we got home I was dreadful upset. Am now.

HARRIS: So was mine, cried all bloody night.

KITTY: I told him I didn't want him to go an' be a soldier, I didn't want to lose him, I didn't want him to go at all! But he said, we have to go, there has to be men to go.

Turns away angrily.

HARRIS: I said to the boss I want to join the army, I want to be released from my job. So he says to me, you know, pompous bloke, 'Look here, Reggie, in the steelworks you are doing just as much for the nation as you would be over there in France.' Well I couldn't see myself catching the bus every morning and all the time my pals were suffering, probably dying, having a laugh somewhere. They were serving their country, weren't they? So I said, 'Look I'm sorry, Mr Roundtree, but I've made up me mind and I have to go.' Well he could see I were determined and he said, 'Go down to wages office and we'll give you what's due, but listen mind, we'll pay you nowt while you're away and we'll not save your job for you either.' 'Thank you,' I said, 'thank you very much,' and joined up with the Lancashires at a bob a day, and you know, I was a very happy man.

KITTY: (*Still angry.*) Everybody thought it'll be over by Christmas. Not me, I thought it would go on at least a year. Most of us thought it couldn't go on longer than that. How could it?

HARRIS: Everyone was going. My pals were going as well, you see? And when you looked at papers and you knew Canadians were coming, Australians were coming, South Africans were coming, there were pictures of all these blokes drilling in Hyde Park in London, or it might be a band playing 'Tipperary', the whole thing were exciting. The other great factor...

Glances at KITTY then looks away, bringing NEWTON more into it.

...was the womenfolk, and that's fifty percent of population believe me...

NEWTON: (*Laughs.*) I'd say!

HARRIS: Some of them were very keen on the war and before too long they were stopping men in the street and handing out white feathers, pushing them into your hand like, if you weren't in uniform.

KITTY: I never gave a white feather, I didn't believe in that! In fact I believed the reverse.

HARRIS: But you see, love, in other words the whole thing was cumulative, we were not pressed, we made our own decisions.

Looks at NEWTON for support.

NEWTON: (*Nods.*) Anxious. I think anxious is the correct word. We were, frankly, anxious to be part of it.

KITTY: It was a madness if you ask me. My sister lived in a village and she told me that every single man in it volunteered in one day, starting at eight-thirty, and there weren't a male between sixteen and sixty left by five o'clock.

HARRIS: They's all went off training, love. See, so far we'd been individualists, so far we'd been Mummy's pet or something like that, and we had will of our own.

Laughs.

Well I did! It were hard to start obeying commands and all that, but we did it, you know, right wheel, left wheel, and all the rest of it. We became a disciplined body of men! Don't laugh. We learned how to make trenches, and we had this sergeant-major who told us fixing bayonets...

Does impression.

'...This is one of the most wonderful things in the army. When I says fix, you don't fix, but when I says bayonets! You whips 'em out and whops 'em on.'

NEWTON: (*Laughs.*) Yes, I've known him.

HARRIS: We've all known him. They gave us these terrible old uniforms, you wouldn't believe it. I didn't fancy them much at all. And within a fortnight we'd been inspected by His Majesty King George the Fifth! Turned out it wasn't only time I'd meet him either. Rumour was we were going to train for six months and then go to Egypt. Well we were in camp for a week when we were told, 'You're leaving tomorrow for "destination unknown". Where was that then? Nobody knew. And we hadn't even got proper webbing, let alone rifles. Didn't matter, by six o'clock in the morning we were on the train, without saying goodbye to anyone. I chucked a postcard out of the window at a station hoping that it would be delivered to my wife. Bloody wasn't. 'Scuse me, love.

He drinks. A slight pause. LAWRENCE TODD comes in. He's an ex-sergeant, everyone's idea of a soldier, square, erect, jutting jaw, very powerful. He's also sensitive, quite shy, sentimental and can be frighteningly emotional. He speaks with a London accent. He carries a glass and a couple of bottles of brown ale.

TODD: Afternoon. They said we could come in here. Todd. Lawrence Todd. BEF.

HARRIS: Sergeant? As was?

TODD: How'd you know?

HARRIS: Could tell by looking at yer. Harris. Private.

TODD: Could tell by looking at yer.

TODD sits, slightly isolated and away from the other. He pours a brown ale. A slight tension between him and HARRIS. KITTY eases it.

KITTY: My sister joined the Women's Emergency Corps. They had to supply their own uniforms and a Grenadier Guardsman came to give them a drill.

A little snigger from HARRIS.

Of course they all were in them hobble skirts then, and he said, 'You lot, you look like a lot of jelly beans!' She had First Aid, Home Nursing and Signalling. Some people didn't like women soldiers though. They thought they were like those suffragettes, chaining themselves up, you know? Getting above themselves. Not me. I thought, who wants to vote anyway?

HARRIS: When we got over to France we were moved up to front in London omnibuses. Don't know how they got them over there. Everybody wanted to get on top in the open because it were a nice day. But we'd not been going very long before it started to rain so we got soaked. Might have known. Pissed on, bloody army, bloody typical. 'Scuse me, love.

KITTY: Swearing's for them who know nowt else.

HARRIS: *(Pulls a face.)* Anyhow got off bus, were lined up, and given this big tot of rum. So in no time we were quite happy. We didn't know where we were going, but the moon broke through the clouds and it was a lovely night. I remember that, the moon. It were alright really.

NEWTON: Not long after I arrived I was introduced to General Joffre, the commander of the entire allied army. He was walking up and down the square with his hands behind his back. He had very light eyes, he was an Albino in fact, and was wearing a black tunic, which fitted extremely badly, sloping outwards over his stomach from the third or fourth button down. He had this extraordinary habit. He'd arrive at headquarters, he'd get out of his car, the Staff would come up to him expecting to be told something, but instead he'd listen to them. I have known cases where he has walked straight back into his car again without uttering a single word.

HARRIS: We spent our first night in a field, quite relaxed, smoking, stretched out, and then we saw this group of French soldiers running up the hillside. There was the sound of gunfire. I think someone laughed it were so strange. Probably me. After a few seconds, there were three explosions. When the smoke cleared we saw the Frenchies picking up one of their own and carry him back down the hill. The shell had killed him, we could see that.

Slight pause.

That was the first time we realised what the war was about. I didn't know what to think.

He moves away again. TODD turns towards them, a little hesitant at joining in.

TODD: When we arrived...

KITTY: Yes?

TODD: They lined the streets. It was Antwerp, I believe. They were jumping up and down.

KITTY: I bet they were.

NEWTON: I heard about the reception in Antwerp.

TODD: They cheered and waved, these Antwerpians or whatever they were, they had the flags out, they went mad. There was flowers and wine and God knows what else.

KITTY: Can imagine.

TODD: The war was young and so were we. Waxing poetical here, alright? I remember the Colonel said, we are gallant, and they are relieved! Ha! Made me laugh that did. We were gallant, they were relieved!

Takes a huge gulp of beer, grins at KITTY.

That's better.

KITTY: You needed that.

TODD: I did.

They're getting on well, NEWTON comes in.

NEWTON: I actually saw Joffre on the afternoon that he decided on the Battle of the Marne. He was sitting astride a hard chair in a dusty little French school courtyard, and was swaying backwards and forwards as he decided what he was going to do. It was an extraordinary thing. I mean very few people can have seen anybody with such a burden placed on his shoulders with nobody to help, just weighing the pros and cons, and what orders to issue. I think it might have been Mons, not Marne.

Checks notebook.

TODD: (*To KITTY.*) Went straight from all that cheering straight to the front. Weren't many of us then. That was the beginning. We were ready alright. We fixed bayonets and said, 'Now come on then! We'll have yer!' Well night come, but not the enemy! There was rifle fire on the left then on the right, and we peered over, but couldn't see nothing. Tell you the truth, we felt neglected. If they was going to fire, what was wrong with us! Hey? We were there, what was wrong with us? And then we got this order! I couldn't believe it. Worst word I ever heard. Retire! We'd hardly got there and we were already retreating!

KITTY: Don't blame you. I'd have done same meself.

TODD: We didn't want to! Listen, you'll like this. Just at the back of our position was a deserted farm and as I went through it I see some pails of milk and I did, I admit it, a most unsoldierly action, I emptied my water bottle and filled it full of milk.

KITTY: Oh most unsoldierly!

HARRIS: I'd have filled mine with beer.

TODD: Well so would I if there was any! Anyhow, we marched for most of the day through this column of refugees. That was a sad sight, everything you could think of: nuns, priests, old girls, most of them had little dog carts and piled up with everything they owned, prams, children, goats, you name it. Finally we stopped by a church and me and my mate saw a couple of young women, so we go over to them thinking we'd have a chat.

KITTY: Oh yes.

TODD: But I see that one of them's got a baby. I says, 'Is your baby all right?' She says, 'It's not my baby. I don't even know its mother, I found it.' What about that? Finding a baby! We give them what we had, some sardines and army biscuits, but then the woman says, 'This baby needs milk.' 'Milk!' I says. 'No problem, Mademoiselle!' I think even the baby was surprised! Ha!

KITTY: Lucky it wasn't beer then.

TODD: Ha! You're right!

Laughs, pause.

Then they told us the retreat was over and so we turned round and were advancing into Belgium on the same road we'd just come up.

He drinks, raising his glass to KITTY as he does so.

HARRIS: We got pulled back an' all. We were by the Marne.

NEWTON: Where?

HARRIS: The Marne.

NEWTON: Ah.

HARRIS: We were marching along this road for what seemed like days, and by this time it were getting very frosty and icy. And it were hard work too. See, we'd already gone two or three weeks without any real sleep, we hadn't had our boots off for all that time either, and we'd had no proper food, nothing hot anyway, bloody army. Anyway, we marched along for a few miles, and men began falling down with tiredness. And the regimental sergeant-major came along with his stick…

TODD turns to look at him.

...and he gave them a walloping till they got up and started marching again. I have to give it to him, he was right, because you couldn't have left them where they were. They'd have frozen to death.

TODD: That's exactly right.

HARRIS: Aye.

He drinks. A pause. TODD leans in to KITTY.

TODD: Listen to this, love, this is not a joke, believe me. We weren't allowed to have white handkerchiefs in case we used them as a white flag! So we had to go and buy red handkerchiefs. That was the first bit of French I learnt, mouchoir rouge. White flag. As if I would.

Then NEWTON, as if out of nowhere:

NEWTON: We were terribly short of hand grenades. I should have told them. Not at Mons. I mean at Neuve Chapelle. Were you there?

HARRIS: Never heard of it.

NEWTON: I don't think they were even invented by then. You see we really needed something to hurl at the enemy. We were so close to them that occasionally we could take pot shots, but to get something actually into a trench was a very different thing. It needed to be hurled up, you see? So it would come down exactly into the trench. In the end we made bombs out of jam tins. I made one or two excursions behind our lines into Armentiere to buy the ingredients. That was the first time in my life I'd been shopping.

KITTY: First time you'd been shopping! I don't believe I'm hearing this!

NEWTON: I quite enjoyed it actually! I was able to find a shop that dealt in explosives and we got some gun cotton and some blasting detonators. I got the farriers to cut up old horse shoes and other bits of old iron and we put the lot into the jam tins. Then we threw them at the Germans. The hand grenade goes off with a terrific explosion and will probably kill or wound all the soldiers in that length of trench. That's why they were so useful.

KITTY: Oh, I see.

NEWTON: Later the war office supplied us with bombs that were exactly the same shape as the old jam tins, they were rather handy things to hold, you see, and you couldn't have had a nicer missile to hurl. We did rather well with them.

HARRIS: Could have done with a few of them ourselves. They told us we were going to attack their trenches in daylight. I'll say this, I was never afraid of dying or being dead, but I was scared stiff of being maimed.

TODD: That's right, absolutely right.

HARRIS: Daylight? They could see you coming, couldn't they? We were ordered to lie down at the edge of this wood and await events. Well we're lying there and two of our own shells burst on our own front line! Doesn't fill you full of confidence does it?

TODD: (*Glance at NEWTON.*) No it doesn't.

HARRIS: There was a lot of screaming, like it was on the air. Then it were quiet. Then we heard this voice out in No-Man's Land, singing as the stars came out.

(*Sings.*) 'O for the wings of a dove.
Far, far away would I rove.'

It was beautiful and clear. He was one of the wounded out there on the battlefield somewhere. Never found him. Shame really, we wanted an encore.

A pause.

TODD: 'Course before we knew where we were, it was Christmas.

KITTY: When it was all supposed to be over.

TODD: By this time we'd stopped marching backwards and had dug ourselves in. It was a terrible winter, but at least everything looked better covered in snow, everything was white, it was beautiful. Then on Christmas day Jerry starts singing a Christmas carol – you know, in German.

Takes out his cigarettes and hands one to HARRIS *who starts singing 'Silent Night' in English.*

And they put up a notice saying Merry Christmas, so we put one up and we started singing too, and when we started, they stopped. And when we stopped, they started.

HARRIS stops singing. They light their cigarettes.

HARRIS: It were easing the way, weren't it, the singing, like coming together, and then this German takes a chance and jumped up on top of the trench and shouted out, 'Happy Christmas, Tommy!' So of course we said 'If he can do it, we can do it,' and we all jumped up. A sergeant-major shouted...

TODD: Get down, you bloody idiots! Ha!

HARRIS: But we said, 'Shut up sergeant, it's Christmas!'

TODD: Then of course we were all up to it. At about 10 in the morning, Jerry's walking across no-man's land with a white flag! Of course, when he gets halfway he stops, waiting for one of us to go out. So we sent a corporal who brought him in, but he didn't blindfold him, and so now our officers had to tell him he was a prisoner of war!

HARRIS: You wouldn't believe it, would you?

TODD: But the Jerry had a message, 'Could we have an armistice of two hours from eleven o'clock till one o'clock?' The colonel agreed it and eleven came and no one was shooting, so one or two of us jumped out on top, while another one or two stopped in the trench with their rifles ready, but they didn't need them. Others followed up and there were scores of us up on top at the finish.

HARRIS: We all went forward to the barbed wire. We could barely reach through it but we managed to shake hands.

TODD: 'Course the officers gave the order...

NEWTON: No fraternisation.

TODD: And then turned their backs on us.

HARRIS: Typical.

TODD: One of the Germans asked me if I knew the Essex
Road in London? Did I know the Essex Road! I told him
my uncle had a shoe repair shop there. He said, there was
a barber shop on the other side of the road where he used
to work. He probably shaved my uncle!

HARRIS: We didn't talk about the war. Just talked about our
families. One of them put a sign up saying, 'Gott mit uns,'
and so we put a sign up saying 'We got mittens too!' I don't
know if they got it.

NEWTON: There was no fraternisation. Our infantry stood
up and strolled about and the Germans did too, but they
never got together or talked to each other at all.

*He glances at the others, they laugh. They're all up now, enjoying
this.*

Well that was the official view.

The others laugh.

HARRIS: My mate Keith had one of their hats on. We were
just walking about, chatting and giving out our names and
addresses for after the war to write to each other. Then
someone got a football out and there we were kicking it
about with them. I scored a goal!

TODD: After a while we started burying our dead. The
Germans did too. We made little crosses out of ration box
wood. We gave some of them to the Germans. They wrote
on theirs, 'Vor Vaterland und Freiheit.' I said, ''Scuse me,
but how can you be fighting for freedom? You started
it, we're the ones who's fighting for freedom.' And this
German said, 'Excuse me English Kamerad, but we are
fighting for freedom for our country.' That was a big shock
to me. I mean I'm not stupid, but I'd never thought that
these blokes felt the same about the war as we did. And
he said, 'It will be over soon because we will win the war
in Russia,' and I said, 'No, no, the Russian steamroller is
going to win the war over there!' 'Well, English Kamerad,
do not let us quarrel on Christmas Day.' I thought I'd leave
it at that.

NEWTON: We had a wonderful Christmas dinner with plum pudding and turkey, I forget how we got hold of it all.

Some reaction from TODD and HARRIS, especially HARRIS.

Then after dinner Motty and I went up on top. My groom was there with my horses and I rode up to within about two hundred yards of the enemy. I dismounted and I gave word to the infantry to keep an eye on me, in case anybody tried any rough business, and I went across and met a small party of them who said, 'Come along into our trenches and have a look at us.' I said, 'No, I'm quite near enough as it is thank you.' And we laughed at each other, and I gave them some English tobacco, and they gave me some German, and then this one fellow said, 'Will you send this off to my girlfriend in Manchester?' So I took his letter and I did, I posted it later.

HARRIS: 'Course in the end we got orders to get back down into the trench.

Glance at NEWTON.

Some of us said, bugger that, and stayed up. So some general behind gave orders for a battery to open fire and that started it all again. We cursed the generals to hell. You want to get up here in this mud you bastards! Never mind you giving orders in your big châteaux and driving about in your big cars!

NEWTON has turned to stare at him.

NEWTON: I don't think that's all they were doing.

TODD: And then there were newspapers in England accusing us of fraternising with the Germans when it had been an armistice!

HARRIS: On Christmas day!

TODD: I wrote back home and told the family, we could do with these patriots writing newspapers out here, and could they stand up in front of us instead of Jerry so we could shoot at them for passing remarks like that while they are nice and tucked up in their English beds calling them Huns or swine. They weren't. We knew what they were. I found out on that day. They were the same as us.

A pause. The mood has soured.

HARRIS: Always the same in't it? Worst enemies are at home.

KITTY: I can't say we had a wonderful Christmas either. He sent word he was coming home on leave. But he didn't come. I missed him. I missed him so much I ached. And the dinner was awful. Can't remember what we had, just remember it was awful.

HARRIS: Back into trench weren't it? Two hours off a year, it were worse than my job, and back to the bloody mud and keeping your head down. You know, all we had to drink was this water with little black things floating around in it.

KITTY: Yuggh.

HARRIS: It was alright, we could boil it up for a nice drop of tea.

KITTY: Lovely.

HARRIS: Should've seen the rats.

KITTY: No thanks.

HARRIS: They lived in corpses.

KITTY: Oh please.

HARRIS: They were as big as cats, I'm not exaggerating, horrible, bloody great things. You put them in a harness, they could have done a milk round.

TODD: And the fleas.

HARRIS: And the fleas. Cheers.

He drinks. They pause.

KITTY: He came back unexpected in the February. By this time I was working in the munitions factory. It was a Monday morning and I was almost ready to go when there was this knocking at the door and this voice shouted, 'Open up, Jerries are here!' And my Mum said, 'Oh, it's him!' And in he came, all mucky, straight from France. And Mum says,

'Oh well – she'll not be going to work then!' And I didn't, I stayed at home all the time he had his leave.

HARRIS: Oh aye.

She acknowledges this with a wry smile.

KITTY: Had to clean him up first. He was filthy, he was lousy an' all! And Mum said, 'You're not sleeping in one of my beds like that. There's a tub in the back. Get them shirts and khaki off and whatnot and I'll see what I can do with it.' We found some old clothes of his that he'd worn before and he had a good rest. But only six days, and he'd spent two of them travelling, so he didn't have very long. The day before he went back he said to me, 'Now Kitty, what would you like for a present? I'm going to buy you something while I'm home.' I said I didn't know, but I did. I was quite vain in those days and I said, 'Oh I've seen a such a beautiful hat in a shop window down the street and I'd like that.' It was nineteen and elevenpence. Well, you could get a lovely hat then for two and eleven! Anyway Percy said, 'Well come on, we'll have a look at it.' And he bought it for me. I'll never forget that hat, it was white felt, and it turned up all around, and with me being dark it looked lovely. Just before he went back, we got dressed up and I took him to the munitions factory and introduced him to Mr Noblet himself. Everyone shook hands with him. And I was so pleased and proud to show him off. And then…then he went back on the Thursday night. I didn't go with him to the tram but he told one of my brothers, 'I'm afraid I shall never come back again.' My brother told me this afterwards. I said, 'Rubbish!'

Slight pause, a change of tone.

Anyway I went back to work and he went back to France.

She seems a little upset, TODD tries to reassure her.

TODD: The trenches you know, in France, were like streets, with one running off the other and little houses and command posts. It was like home from home, which would have made your husband happy. We even had this row of cottages running across at right angles to the line of trenches, running across both of them. So, up this end was our cottages and the Germans moved in to the ones at their end. This is true, we were next door neighbours!

She smiles.

There were about ten of us in our house and when we were in the kitchen we could hear Jerry through the wall. We had a backyard too with another wall between us and them. One of the corporals sat up in the bedroom with a rifle taking potshots at any of them who wandered out into their yard. Jerry shouted over, 'I know Croydon better than any of you!' 'Course then a Croydon bloke started arguing the point. It was very friendly like that with our neighbours. One day we were in our little house, cooking our stew on the fire when Jerry decides to have a bit of fun. He fires at the chimney of our cottage and knocks one or two bricks down into the fire. The bloody stew went all over the floor! We could hear Jerry laughing. He could hear us see? And knew he'd picked the right time see, and he decided to have a go at our bloody stew! Well we weren't having that, were we? The Royal Engineers came into our house and dug a tunnel under the German end. I reckon they took enough gun cotton down there to blow up Paris. We cleared out and left them too it. 'Whoosh!' The whole row went up in blue flames, along with the end house where Jerry was. Teach him to knock out our stew!

He gets up. Then NEWTON speaks to KITTY.

NEWTON: Our redoubt on the front line was regarded as rather a showpiece. My CO brought several people up to see it, amongst them Sir Henry Rawlinson, who I'd known in peace-time, actually he'd seen me win a point to point on Salisbury Plain.

Stifled laugh from HARRIS.

Then to my surprise General Haig himself came up, and while I was showing him round, the Germans started shelling. One of his staff officers got very fussed about this and said, 'Hurry up, let's get the Commander away.' But Haig took no notice and went on, even slower than before if possible, and asked me questions, then he slowly walked off down the communication trench, quite unmoved.

HARRIS: Haig? General Haig! Nothing!

NEWTON: I beg your pardon.

HARRIS: Listen to this. We got these orders to clean up as we were going to be inspected by someone high up. We didn't know who but we made ourselves fairly presentable and next morning marched for about fifteen miles until we came to a little valley with a road running along the bottom of it. There were a lot of other units already assembled and we waited there for three or four hours, then along came these staff cars and all these high-ups got out and proceeded to mount their horses which were waiting for them. One of them was the King. And I don't mean one of the horses! As I stand here, it was the King. Told you, second time I met him, see? He rode along the first three or four ranks. Our instructions had been that at the conclusion of the parade we were to put our caps on the points of our bayonets and wave and cheer. So that's what we did – 'Hip, hip, hoo bloody ray'. Soon as we did it, the King's horse reared up and he fell off on his arse!

Laughter from TODD and KITTY.

NEWTON: I'd ask you, if you don't mind, to show some respect.

HARRIS: Anyway. They put him back in his car. Safer, I reckon. Then we all sang 'Rule Britannia' as he drove off.

Awkward pause.

KITTY: We sang too. We sang all the time while we were making the shells. You know, I didn't hear one grumble in all the time I was in that factory, and hardly ever heard of one woman that stayed home because she had her man in mind. We all had that didn't we?

Stops for a second.

I was working with some sailors' wives from ships that sank. It was pitiful to see them, so we 'ad to cheer them up as best we could, so that's when we sang.

HARRIS sings a bit of a sentimental ballad.

It was beautiful to listen to. I've never seen women work like it in my life before or since. It was just magic, like one big happy family.

She regards HARRIS for a second and listens to his song. He plays up to her, singing beautifully. He stops.

We didn't sing that, but it was like it.

HARRIS: We had Cornet Joe over in the German front line. He was famous. He used to play his cornet for us. We'd shout out, 'Give us another one, Joe!' And he'd yell and ask us what we wanted to hear and we'd say, 'Give us the old Bull and Bush.' So he'd play it and we we'd sing it. You could forget there was a war on. And there were some who did, and before they knew it they'd got a bullet through their head sitting on the bloody khasi.

TODD: Ha!

KITTY: Please. If you don't mind!

HARRIS: Sorry love.

KITTY: I want some more tea anyway.

She gets up and goes out.

HARRIS: Sorry love.

Grins.

Tea! If only she knew. You could forget there was a war on if you'd had your rum.

TODD: I used to give it out! I had this big tablespoon and mess tin full of it. I'd go along the trench, 'Open up!' And I'd pour this tablespoon full of rum down their throats! Like Mummy!

Checks to see that KITTY has gone.

Course there were other considerations.

HARRIS: (*Smirks, raises glass.*) To other considerations.

TODD: I had this man called Sam. He was short and stumpy and about the ugliest man I've ever seen. One time we saw him walk up to a cottage on top of a hill. Didn't know why. Later on we found out he had an agreement with this little lady up there. When she hung her clothes on the line it meant her old man had gone out! And when the signal came you couldn't hold Sam back – he was up there like a jack rabbit.

HARRIS: They all wanted it.

TODD: Who? The men?

HARRIS: No, the women.

TODD: Ha! For a price. They used to put a sign in their window saying, 'Washing done here for soldiers.' I've seen twenty men waiting in one room to have their washing done, and there were probably others upstairs!

HARRIS: All waiting with their washing.

They laugh. TODD leans in. He and HARRIS are sitting close.

TODD: Afterwards, you know, these women used to sit on the end of the bed, open their legs and flick this brownish stuff around between them, ready for the next man.

HARRIS: How'd you know about that?

TODD laughs.

You ever get to Armentières? It weren't a big place. We got into the estaminets and we were drinking vin blanc, of course.

TODD: Of course.

Both glance at NEWTON who isn't looking but listening.

HARRIS: This estaminet I was in, this particular night, it were absolutely crowded and there were five women in there and it was five francs a time if you went with them, up the stairs and in the bedrooms. And fellows were going in, coming out, queueing up again, going in, coming out, I couldn't believe it. My mate said, 'You going up?' I said:

'No. Not with them things.' They were all sorts of ages, the women, and you know, the first thing she does is grab your five franc note.

TODD: Your what?

HARRIS: Your five franc note! Wait for it. Then she unfastens your flies and has a feel and squeezes it, sees if there's anything wrong with it. Then she just throws this cloak off and she's on the bed, you know, ready for you.

TODD: How'd you know about that?

HARRIS: I was told! No I didn't go up there, as I sit here. I was there though one time when the padre walked in. 'Have none of you any mothers? Have none of you sisters? I shall report this to the colonel.' 'What, having no sisters?' He didn't laugh. He reduced our time out of the line. Makes you wonder, doesn't it, how many more people were killed to stop them queueing up for a woman. I didn't fancy them though. You didn't know what you were going to get.

NEWTON moves over to them.

NEWTON: I remember the case of the captain who applied for special leave. On his chit he was asked for his reason. He put quite boldly, sexual starvation. And to everyone's surprise and delight he got his leave and went off to Paris to indulge himself!

TODD and HARRIS laugh.

Lord Kitchener wasn't so happy about it, of course. He issued a memo. He said that in recent months quite a number had rendered their selves unfit for duty through negligence in contracting venereal disease. They tried everything including a German system called 606 which necessitated an injection of mercury into the system. Very painful I imagine. Apparently it worked better if you sweated it out. So you could see a lot of men running around pretending they were keeping themselves fit!

KITTY comes back in with another cup of tea as he says this. NEWTON doesn't notice.

But nothing worked until Kitchener issued a second memo. 'The victim's parents or his wife would be immediately notified in the future if any man rendered himself unfit through contracting VD.'

KITTY coughs NEWTON looks round.

Ah. I beg your pardon.

Smiles at TODD and HARRIS.

That stopped it quicker than any 606, I can tell you!

TODD and HARRIS laugh.

TODD: We needed it.

KITTY: Needed what?

TODD: Whatever it took, dear.

KITTY: Whatever what took?

TODD: To get you through it.

KITTY: (*Angry.*) It weren't exactly easy back here, you know? Munitions workers were just about the lowest form of life. We were supposed to be making a great deal of money. Well that was rubbish and people had all sorts of nasty things to say, but it were really dangerous. I was filling eighteen pounders in the shell-filling shed. There was explosions all the time. We'd hear, 'Oh, so and so's gone.' Perhaps she'd made a mistake and her eye was out. That wasn't nice was it?

HARRIS: No that wasn't nice.

KITTY: And what about the chemicals we had to deal with? They were in the powder and they made you go yellow. Our skin became perfectly yellow, right down through the body, legs and toenails even. Perfectly yellow. Sometimes it caused a rash. You had a horrible rash all round the chin.

Still irritated by them.

You can laugh, we were a bevy of beauties, you know, and we objected to having yellow beards! And the hair! If it was fair or brown it went a beautiful gold but if it was any grey, it went grass-green! And washing wouldn't do anything – it only made it worse.

HARRIS: I'll tell you about chemicals.

KITTY: You weren't there.

HARRIS: I was. It were a beautiful day.

KITTY: What were?

HARRIS: It were a perfect day, a perfectly yellow day. I was lying in a field writing a letter to me mother, the sun was shining, and I remember a lark singing high up in the sky. Then, suddenly, there was this sort of slight bombardment. Nothing much, a couple of shells a few hundred yards in front of us. We didn't take much notice. Then we saw it. This green cloud coming slowly down towards us. One of our boys was a chemist and he passed the word along that this was chlorine. He told us, 'If you piss on your handkerchiefs and hold them to your mouths, it will save your lungs anyway.'

TODD: I saw it. I saw these men come running down from the front. I've never seen anyone so bloody terrified in my life. They were tearing at their throats and their eyes were glaring out like they were going mad. One chap had his hand blown off, and his wrist was fumbling around, tearing at his throat. That was the most the most grotesque thing I ever saw.

HARRIS: It formed a sort of foamy liquid in your lungs, which more or less drowned you. A lot of them died pretty quickly, drowning in the air.

Suddenly very angry.

On this beautiful fucking day! Sorry, sorry. Excuse me.

KITTY looks at him sympathetically. She sits down.

KITTY: It's alright.

TODD: I got it too. It got your eyes, they were streaming with water, and all we had was a roll of bandages in the first aid kit. So we bandaged each other's eyes, and anyone who could see would lead a line of half a dozen or so of us. There were lines and lines of us with rolls of bandages around our eyes, moving back towards Ypres.

HARRIS: Day after it happened, Sir John French came up and praised us for our bravery. We just thought what did he know about it? Why didn't he stay in his office?

Harsh look at NEWTON.

TODD: Took me three months to recover.

He stops. A silence. A sense of hostility towards NEWTON.

KITTY: Well.

NEWTON: One of my men absented himself from the front line you know?

He looks at the others.

I'd like to say this if you don't mind. He'd done it on two occasions once a battle had started, and after it was over he came back and made some excuse that he'd mislaid the way. Well, of course, I realised that this was a very serious offence and the first time it happened I sentenced him to some severe punishment myself, but the second time I realised he must be sent up to headquarters. They court martialled him and sentenced him to death by firing squad.

He pauses.

The Colonel set me the unpleasant task of attending the shooting and pinning onto this soldier's heart a piece of coloured flannel to give the marksmen something to fire at. His name was Stanley, John Stanley.

HARRIS: You don't have to do it. That's a fact. It's the one thing you can refuse to do. You can refuse to be in a firing squad. You've got an absolute right!

NEWTON: He was to be shot at dawn and I lay awake thinking of it all night and I thought I'd try and help him a bit, so I took down a cupful of brandy and gave it to him and said 'Drink this and you won't know very much about it.' He said, 'What is it?' I said, 'It's brandy.' He said, 'Well, I've never drunk spirits in my life, there's no point in my starting now.' That to me was a sort of spurious courage in a way. Two men came and led him out of the hut where he'd been guarded all night. As he left the hut his legs gave way, then I, then one could see how frightened he was. Rather than marching to the firing spot he was dragged along. When we got to the wall he had his hands tied behind his back, his eyes were bandaged and the firing squad were given the order to fire. Only, two of the eight men had their rifles loaded. The others fired blanks so that they wouldn't actually know who had fired the fatal shot.

HARRIS: You can always tell! You know by the recoil if it was loaded with ball or not. You would know if you killed him.

NEWTON: I wondered at the time 'What on earth will happen if they miss him and don't kill him completely?' I was very anxious about that because I thought I might have to shoot him myself. When they fired he fell to the ground writhing as all people do. Even if they've been killed they have this reflex action of writhing about which goes on for some minutes. Then he died, so I didn't have to shoot him with my revolver.

NEWTON is clearly upset by what he's revealed.

TODD: Not right is it, Englishmen shooting Englishmen. I thought we were in France to fight the bloody Germans.

NEWTON: I just wanted to say, it wasn't so easy for any of us.

There's a silence finally broken by HARRIS.

HARRIS: I say, I say, I say. You hear the one about?

He stops and begins to sing. The others join when they feel like it.

'They were summoned from the hillside,
they were called in from the glen,
and the country found them ready
at the stirring call for men.
Let no tears add to their hardships
as the soldiers pass along,
and although your heart is breaking,
make it sing this cheery song.'

ALL: 'Keep the home fires burning,
　　While your hearts are yearning.
　　Though the lads are far away,
　　they dream of home.
　　There's a silver lining,
　　Through the dark clouds shining.
　　Turn the dark cloud inside out,
　　Till the boys come home.'

HARRIS: 'Overseas there came a pleading,
　　help a nation in distress…'

Stops.

Don't know anymore.

Slightly embarrassed laughter. A different mood, getting darker.

KITTY: It got worse, just got worse and worse, didn't it? One time I went into butcher's shop and I said, 'That looks like cat.' And he said, 'It is cat.' Well I couldn't face that. And I missed him more and more as it went on. I used to look in the paper every day at the casualty lists. You always found people in them you knew. That were depressing, and then everybody wore black, and that was even more depressing. Black, black, black everywhere.

HARRIS: I remember sitting on this bank, grass bank, it were just before the Somme.

KITTY: That's the one. The Somme.

The beginning of a low sound, a background rumble, hardly heard.

HARRIS: We were just sitting there, this were evening and the sun were going down, it was very warm, and suddenly there was this bloody great swarm of huge beetles, each one about an inch long, coming from the enemy side, swarming down the bank. Where they'd come from or where they were going I don't know, but they never deviated, swarming in a straight line about three yards across they were. In the end we moved to either side of them. It were a stream of millions. They marched along for hours. Running away I reckon.

KITTY: We read about it in the Evening News. I remember reading it out loud to me mother.

TODD: (*Getting tense.*) It was coming, we all knew it. We were up there, waiting for it, thinking about it. The chaplain came over to me and asked if I was scared? I told him the truth, what else could I say? He said, would I'd like to pray with him? Well I wasn't a praying man, but I said, yes I would. The other buggers sniggered about it, but I told them exactly what I'd said to God, and that was I wanted him to save me. That shut them up. I think they felt a bit jealous. You see, because I'd prayed, they thought God would be more on my side than their's. Ha! I saw a couple of them later, kneeling in the water trying to catch up.

KITTY: I remember reading the number of dead. It were nineteen thousand.

NEWTON: Just before the battle, I was made a company commander. It was a great responsibility but that, of course, never worried me.

He's perhaps a little too sure about this.

I think it was Mrs Sidney Webb who said, 'There are people in England who are born to give orders and there are people who are born to take them.' It's true, isn't it? A boy in a public school, he's had two years as a fag and another four or five years going on up the school, and he either was or wasn't selected to be a house prefect. I mean, I had command of a couple of hundred men. That proved it, didn't it? You ran your own show. I did anyway.

He turns away for a moment as if he's doubting this.

TODD: We were all getting nervous. There's no doubt about that. Most of us had been up at Ypres and we knew what we had to do.

Sudden anger.

And what they were asking us to carry into battle was bloody ridiculous! I asked the commander, I said it

35

respectful though I didn't feel it, if it was possible for me to load up a major to make my point. The commander said I certainly could. So I got two privates to put everything on this major: bombs in the pockets, sandbags, spade, kit, rations, extra ammunition round the neck – all of it. Then I said, 'How does that feel?' He said, ' Well, It's a hell of a weight'. So I said, 'You haven't even started yet. You forgot the rifle, and you've also got a pannier which weighs forty-six pounds in your other hand. Here you are.' So he picks them up and he's groaning under the weight and I says, there's a farm field at the back of here that's just been ploughed – try walking 100 yards and see how you feel. He said, 'You feel very strongly about this, don't you?' And I said, 'Wouldn't you? Wouldn't bloody anybody?'

NEWTON: We'd moved up to a marvellous château close to the front line. The night before the attack the brigadier insisted on us having an old-fashioned mess dinner.

HARRIS: Dinner.

NEWTON: At seven o'clock promptly we sat at a large table and the wine was brought round in decanters.

TODD: Decanters.

NEWTON: I can remember my delight at finding an old gramophone. After dinner I played Puccini.

TODD/HARRIS: Puccini!

NEWTON: And I drank whisky. I imagine I felt very sorry for myself. I hardly slept. At five-thirty in the morning I heard a curious noise in the sky overhead. It seemed to me that it was just as if some giants were carrying huge strips of canvas and ripping them apart.

TODD: The guns.

NEWTON: Yes. It was our bombardment to soften them up. It had started. I can only say that I began to be excited. It's hard to believe now. The noise rose to a crescendo such as I'd never heard before. The effect of it created a sort of hysterical feeling.

HARRIS: Aye, bloody hysterical.

TODD and NEWTON are standing by now facing each other across the stage.

NEWTON: One's instinct was to go with the chaps, and so to see what was going on. On the other hand, we'd been warned over and over again that officers' lives must not be thrown away – in fact we'd been told that officers should lead from behind and only go forward when the attack had lost its impetus. And that's what I tried to do.

TODD: Hmmph!

NEWTON: That's what I was ordered to do.

TODD: We were assembled at one in the morning and crossed over in the dark to a jumping off trench in No-Man's Land. We waited in it until quarter to six, standing there in dead silence, you couldn't make a noise, and the fellow next to you felt like your best friend, you loved him, although you probably didn't know him a day before. They were the longest and shortest hours of my life. Some of them were crying. We knew what we going into, see?

NEWTON: I know.

(*Quiet.*) I was going round prodding my men. 'Couple of minutes, you watch me for the signal to go over the top,' You're so busy telling them what to do you haven't time to think about yourself. 'Get your pack on. Hurry up. Get your bayonet fixed. Have you got a bomb in your pocket? It's better to carry a bomb than money. How many bullets have you got?' All that kind of thing. You never have enough time.

TODD: As soon as it was light, I issued a big ration of rum. They told us we were going to receive orders to advance at any moment. That moment was a long time coming I can tell you, and everyone got very jittery.

KITTY: Nineteen thousand dead, it said. That were just the first day. July the first, nineteen sixteen. I remember it. I had a day off.

TODD: It was just five minutes to go – then zero – and all hell let loose. Our barrage, then the German, which was a dirty orange colour and left horrible fumes.

NEWTON: Here we go!

TODD: The whistle blew.

NEWTON: We went up. I looked over to the left and there were the London Scottish who were on our left, running forward.

TODD: Over the top we went. Some of us had ladders and some just got out as best they could, slipping up the mud and their packs pulling them back.

NEWTON: The London Scottish vanished into the smoke and there was nothing left but noise.

TODD: We kept on in extended order, each man about a yard apart.

NEWTON: We saw nothing and we knew nothing. We lived in a world of noise, simply noise.

TODD: I didn't feel fear, not then, the fear had left me. I was like an animal with this great shell on my back pushing forward. I didn't look, I saw. I didn't listen, I heard. And my nose was full of stench and fumes and death and I could taste the top of my mouth, and I breathed it all in. I was like an animal. I could feel the rifle hard in my hands. It's up at port with the bayonet into the sky. There's just a line of us going forward and the shells are a blur, you could see them in the air. In the first two minutes we do a hundred yards, you're having to go round the shell holes, see, and you're keeping the line straight and there's some casualties, so there's gaps coming in the line.

(*Suddenly he roars.*) Straighten that bloody line!

This is happening to him now.

The first two, three hundred yards there wasn't too much firing and we're only losing ten or fifteen that I can see, but as soon as we we're within a hundred yards of them they open up with the machine guns. I can feel the bullets as

they go past, hear them whip and whine and the air move.
You just go forward, and from that point on you don't get
no more orders. Then I'm twenty yards from their trench.
And the bullets are louder, faster, all around you, the
noise is fucking incredible, and I shout, 'Charge!' And I
bring my rifle down facing them, and I'm thinking you're
getting it now, you bastards! So I'm under their wire and
down into their trench. And there's two of them running
and one turns back with his rifle up, and I'm on him and
it's in! The bayonet's in! I watch his face as he goes down,
he's staring at me like he doesn't know who I am, but
he does know who I am, and we're in this together, and
I pull it out fast and turn it to use the butt on the second
one, but he ain't having none of it, and he's got his hands
up and yelling, 'Kamarad! Mercy Kamarad!' And there's
Johnny Cole behind me, who's got it in the shoulder, and
he's got a pistol from somewhere and he points it straight
at this German who's got his hands up and he pulls the
trigger, but he must have jerked it because he missed, and
this German is on the bottom of the trench screaming for
mercy, and Johnny's pointing the pistol again, but I give
him a shove. I can see the blood on my bayonet, and I
says, 'No, he won't do any harm.' I put a man in charge
of him and go forward to clear the rest of the trench. At
the next bay I stop and take cover while Johnny throws a
grenade and as soon as it's exploded I go in to see if there's
any left.

Pause.

There's no one, except a dead one who we didn't kill, and
we go all the way along. No one. They'd all pulled back to
their second line.

Pause.

So that meant we'd do it all over again tomorrow.

NEWTON: I found a sergeant lying dead on the ground with his
hand on an open bible. It was a Douai bible and from that
I knew he was a Catholic. I thought perhaps I would write
to his parents.

A silence. HARRIS gets up, comes forward, breaking the mood, in his way, challenging both NEWTON and TODD.

HARRIS: I had a wish. My wish was for a nice fresh wound.

TODD: I hated bloody conchies!

HARRIS: Course there's wounds and there's wounds. You had to take the chance, you could get blown to bits, or a leg off. Or you'd get, 'Yes mate, you've got a bloody perfect wound there, it'll get you to Blighty alright, only thing is, it's infected.' That's no good is it? Tubes in here, tubes in there, dying of poison at the end of it all. Oh no, what I wanted was a lovely, bright sparkling, clean wound, preferably in the upper arm or the buttock was the ticket.

TODD: All the conchies. The religious ones, the political ones, and the ones who didn't want to bother!

HARRIS: I tried to do it for myself. I was in a shell-hole and I heard an ammunition wagon coming up and I thought, I'll put my leg under the wheel and say it was an accident. As it got closer I began to stretch me leg over, but you know, I couldn't do it. I didn't even had the bloody guts to break me own leg.

TODD: I saw this conchie in a cell once. He said, 'People of the world unite, you have nothing to lose but your chains.' That stayed on my mind. He refused to put on the khaki. I had to force it on him, and then take him out to a compound and leave him there all night, but he took it off again and shredded it and hung it on the barbed wire. He sat there all night naked and freezing to death.

HARRIS: I had to wait. I knew it would come. And it did. There were about ten of us on this hill, you see, and we had the wind up, and a staff officer on a horse come to us and said, 'Now men, I want you to stand firm. You've got a good position, you should be alright.' But we all said, 'We've no chance, sir, whatsoever, the Germans are coming up.' So he started appealing,'Men of the East Lancs, you've got a good reputation.' I said, 'It's not much good here, is it sir?' And just at that moment the Germans came up the hill and started firing. Well, that did it. We all run away. And

so did the officer on his horse. In the end I found myself in
this wood on my own. I saw this empty cottage and went
in. It were strange, the coffee on the stove was still warm,
and there was bread on the table. I didn't touch none of
it. I knew this was my time, see? I came out and couldn't
believe my eyes. There was this trench full of French
territorials I hadn't even noticed. One of them turned
round to me and went, 'Sshhh.' I nodded, don't worry,
pal. And then suddenly, one of them shouted, 'We're
surrounded, get out,' and threw his machine gun away.
There was a stampede as we all rushed down this trench
and that's when the Germans came throwing bombs. I
remember going up in the air and landing on the ground.
When I came round I was in this sort of clearing station
and hearing these Scotch voices of the nurses. I wasn't in
any pain but I could see that shrapnel had gone into my
kneecap. It was a joy, what a bloody joy! This chaplain
came up and he was trying to comfort me. He told me that
he had some relatives that had been out there from the
beginning and by God's grace they hadn't had a scratch.
He said, they've been lucky, haven't they? I tried not to
laugh.

TODD: I felt ashamed of how I'd treated that conchie.

HARRIS: Home! Bloody home!

KITTY: My other sister was in VAD in a hospital in Bingley.
She said, the men used to come and say, it were hell. There
were a few more adjectives with it, but that were their
word, it's hell. They were all shell-shocked, which meant
that they couldn't keep their heads still, or their hands still.
She had to write their letters. I went down to see her and
did a few letters myself. Most of them couldn't say what
they wanted, or they were too shy to tell me, so I wrote
them as if I was writing to him. 'My dearest darling,' you
know, and 'forever yours'. And other things. They thought
the letters were wonderful. It worked for me too. You see I
hadn't heard from him for a few months.

Pause.

We were very, very proud of our boys, all of them, and wanted to give them everything we had, including our love letters.

HARRIS: We were bloody heroes! I'd never seen anything like it. When we came out of Manchester station they had to have coppers on horseback to hold the crowd back. The stretcher cases went into ambulances and the rest of us went in civilian cars. I was in a Sunbeam open tourer! We were mobbed as we drove through the city. I had the time of my life in that hospital. When we were convalescing we used to go down in the town of an evening. Couldn't buy a drink!

NEWTON: I didn't like going home. They hadn't any conception of what it was like, and on occasions when I did talk about it, my father would argue points of fact that he couldn't possibly have known about. They seemed to feel that the war was one long cavalry charge; that we spent all day and all night chasing Germans or they chased us. And of course the general idea was that England couldn't lose. And you couldn't get through to the women either. If they didn't say the right thing I'd get annoyed. As a matter of fact I was relieved to go back to people who understood what it was like. Home wasn't very real anymore, I'm afraid.

KITTY: We could see you trying to be as cheerful as you could and not saying much about anything. We knew how bad all the mud and the dirt was, but what could we say? We could see you wanted to go back.

HARRIS: I got another white feather! I did! I were out of hospital and in an old suit on a bus, when this woman leaned over and gave me a feather and said, 'Here's a gift for a brave soldier.' I took it off her and said, 'Thank you very much, I need one of those.' Then I took my pipe out of my pocket and put this feather down the stem and worked it like a pipe cleaner. When I'd finished, it were right filthy I pulled it out and said, 'You know we didn't get these in the trenches,' and handed it back to her. She dropped the feather and bloody near fell over in her hurry to get off the bus. I sat back and bloody laughed.

KITTY: Some of them said they wanted to go back because they wanted to finish it. That's what they said.

HARRIS: Instead of sending us straight back to the front they sent us back to Étaples to retrain. I'd only been in near three bloody years so they had us marching around this bullring for days.

TODD: Better than Flanders.

HARRIS: There were a colonel who stood on a rostrum until he'd inspected every detachment and if he didn't like your marching, he sent you to the back of the column like a lot of naughty schoolboys.

TODD: Better than the mud.

NEWTON: Passchendaele was the final horror.

HARRIS: There was this sergeant who had a VC. He were a real cockney. He said, 'Nah I'm gonna give you a lecture on "esprit de corps". If you is in the canteen and I come in, and you say, "What you gonna have, sergeant?" That's esprit de corps!'

NEWTON: It was beyond anything I've ever seen.

TODD: A regiment only went up for forty-eight hours, they couldn't keep them there any longer.

HARRIS: I was there! I was bloody there!

TODD: There wasn't even a front line. It was another world, a landscape of mud, ten foot deep, full of rotting animals and corpses. There were a few posts every now and again scraped out of it, like holes in the slime that kept running back in. The only way out was on duckboards which they shelled. You couldn't go left or right off the boards or you drowned in the mud and corpses, so you had to keep on going facing the shells.

HARRIS: Let's face it, there was no chance of getting a Blighty at Passchendaele.

Silence.

TODD: The guns were caked in the mud. They looked like the boughs of trees. You were just a sodden mud man scraping it out of your eyes to see where you were going.

A silence.

HARRIS: Dead bodies smell sweet. Then there was the smell of peardrops, which was the chlorine, off the gas, it got released out of the ground any time a shell broke things up. Actually, you know, it smelt better than peardops.

A silence.

NEWTON: I had never seen so many dead men. I thought to myself, 'All the world's dead – they're all dead.' That's all I could think. I even saw one up a tree. A corpse I mean. I don't know how it got up the tree.

Pause.

It was as if civilisation had ended. I've never seen anything as beautiful as that battlefield.

HARRIS: Should have seen the latrines. It was like people had sicked up their guts. I dug one once. We took Casey to it. He had dysentery. It were terrible. He was crawling about, his trousers round his feet, his backside hanging out, his shirt all shitty. He couldn't even walk. I took him by one arm and someone else got hold of him by the other, and we lowered him down trying to turn him round and put his backside towards the trench. But he slipped out of our hands and slid down head first into the slime. We didn't have enough strength to pull him out, and he couldn't help himself at all. We did finally get him out, but he was dead. He'd drowned in his own shit.

A silence.

NEWTON: Then it started again. Passchendaele.

He writes the word in his notebook, agitated.

HARRIS: It went off with a bang, didn't it? They'd sapped out under the German lines and packed two hundred ton of high explosive in a tunnel. Went up seven in morning. It

were incredible. I saw this whole village lifting up out of
the earth, as slow as anything, and whole houses splitting
and falling apart high up in the air. The sky was full of it,
huge trees were going up, their roots turning upside down,
and when they reached the top they disintegrated into bits
and pieces and dust and clouds, and although we were so
far away, we got pieces of brick and masonry falling into
the trench around us.

TODD: Shells came down all the time, day and night. Some of
my boys got hysterical. Even the rats got hysterical.

NEWTON: In a flash of time, a fifth of a second, you'd decide
that the shell you could hear coming was the one for you.
You'd throw yourself down into the mud. Then you'd
realise it wasn't for you and it would go sailing busily on
and plonk down on somebody else four hundred yards
away. The shell had been for them! You'd wait a second
or two then you'd get up and roar with laughter, and the
others would laugh at you for having been the first one
to throw yourself down. This of course was hysterics. It
bocomon a kind of game. The first person in a group who
shows a sign of fear by giving way and taking cover – he'd
lose a point and it counted against him. The one who held
out longest had gained a point. It went on all the time, this
game. But what on earth was it for?

He's feeling disturbed by this.

HARRIS: We were waiting for the whistle to go up and there's
a bloke bending down by the firestep who calls out,
'Overture and beginners please!' So I said, 'Bloody actor!'
And he said, 'At your service, sir,' and bows. And over the
top he went.

TODD: I slid down into this shell-hole and saw a hare running
around, zigzagging with its eyes bulging out with fear,
but it wasn't half as scared as I was. I didn't move, just
stayed there with me head down till I saw I was the only
one left of all us. I was still there when it got dark. It had
started to rain and I'd slid about ten foot down to the
bottom. I flashed my torch around and saw I was next to

a dead German. I thought, Christ, I can't spend the night
with him, so I went to get out of the hole. But every time
I climbed up I slid back down the sides. I tried again but
couldn't get out. I tried again. Still couldn't get out. Then I
realised I was starting to sink into the mud.

*He stops for a second, pushing down the panic that's rising in
him.*

TODD: I started to shout out for some help. I didn't care if it
was Germans who heard me. I was yelling out, 'Help me!'
I didn't panic usually, but my boots got stuck and I realised
I was sinking further and further down into the water at
the bottom. And all the time this German was looking
at me with his dead eyes. I shoved him under the water
and tried to climb up on him but I was still sinking all the
time! I shouted, I screamed, I shone my torch up into the
air. Help me! No one came and I could see they wouldn't
till morning, and by this time I was waist deep in the
water and still going down. So I didn't know what to do. I
decided I would sing.

The feelings arising from this are very strong.

I sang hymns. I cursed, I raved. I went mad. And I prayed.
But I was still sinking further and further down and the
water got up to my chest. I jammed my rifle into the side
of the hole and wrapped the sling round my arm and just
held on. The bottom of my body was completely paralysed
with the cold, and I could feel the water creeping a little
bit further up, and a little bit further up until it was over
my armpit and on to my shoulder. I hung on just trying
to keep my head out of it. The Germans starting shelling
again, and I prayed for one, because I thought I'd sooner
be killed with a shell than die drowning in bloody filthy
mud and water!

Pauses.

I don't know how I got through that night. Then I thought
I was dreaming and I see this head on the edge of the pit
and it says, 'Hang on, hang on chum.' It was all because
of the shelling in the night, you see? It had saved me. It

had broken the telephone wires and a signaller had come looking to mend them. That was about it. That was about as much as I could take.

Very close to tears.

It was done for me then.

HARRIS: I saw someone in a shell-hole like that. It were a kid up to his neck in it. I called down to him, 'Are you hit, son?' He said, 'Yes, I am a little.' But there was no hope, was there? He was in this sea of mud. I saw a little sapling in a bit of a copse that we were supposed to be using as our front line and I tried to bend it over to him, but he couldn't reach it. He was only a boy. Nothing I could do.

TODD shakes his head.

TODD: I crawled back. The men were like a flock of sheep lying in a field. Some of them cried out for water. And one of them grabbed my legs. I shook him off. I didn't give him any water. I crawled away.

He looks at HARRIS who doesn't say anything. A silence.

NEWTON: I always felt that someone up above was ordering things, and that he, or whoever it was, probably knew more about it than I did. Of course I realised it was mainly the fear of fear, I suppose, the fear of being found afraid, being found out. We had an obsessive interest in who would come out of it best. Everybody started talking about fate and mind-readers and even psychics. There was a sergeant who knew things. I remember he suddenly said, 'Lieutenant Stewart's been killed.' Almost immediately, a man came from the front trench and told us that Lieutenant Stewart had indeed been killed by a nose cap that ripped his spine. During the next two weeks this sergeant had the same feeling about others who also died. We called him Hoodoo Bill which he didn't like, and so he stopped telling us these things. After a while he became a nervous wreck. Because he was suppressing it all, I suppose. I was in a shell hole with my friend, Mepham, and he started reciting 'The Skylark', by Shelley. I found myself frantically yelling out 'Stop!' I knew that if he'd gone on, I don't know what would have happened to my nerve.

Beginning to crack.

I don't know why I was so upset. I was hardly ever without the poems of Siegfried Sassoon. I'd gone up to Passchendaele with one or two of them in my haversack.

He's trying to control his shaking hands. HARRIS turns to KITTY.

HARRIS: Sometimes your officer was a bit of a clot and you had to look after him.

KITTY: Did you?

HARRIS: Oh yes, I mean the ordinary disgruntled, perpetual grouser like me would be looking after the officer.

Looks sympathetically at NEWTON.

NEWTON: Would you? I mean, would you really? Is that how you felt about it?

HARRIS: Don't worry about it.

A silence. KITTY turns as ex-rifleman JOE HAINES comes in. He's an American, a happy man, full of optimism and bonhomie.

HAINES: Sir? Do you mind?

HARRIS: No. Come in.

HAINES: Haines, Joe Haines.

HARRIS: Kidder Harris. Yank?

They shake hands.

HAINES: Sure. Colorado. Ma'am.

He takes off his raincoat. He is dressed in well-cut, new looking American clothes.

KITTY: (*Impressed.*) Pleased to meet you.

HAINES: And you ma'am.

He nods a greeting to the others.

What a day, huh? I've just been telling them about St Nazaire, France.

KITTY: Aye?

HAINES: That's where we arrived.

KITTY: We'd been waiting for you. Been waiting for years.

HAINES: We knew that, ma'am.

KITTY: We were starving over here, you know?

HAINES: I told them. First thing we did was parade through the town. The people went crazy.

KITTY: I'll bet.

HAINES: You should have seen them. They lined the streets and even the gutters. They were delirious with joy. The girls jumped into our ranks and threw flowers and even kissed you, and screamed, they screamed a lot. And I guess they must have admired us a lot too.

KITTY: We had no food, you see? Factories weren't making pork pies, just shell cases and bullets.

HAINES: We never imagined anything like it, you know, that we'd be welcomed so warmly. See, they thought the war was going to end because of us. We were just young fellers and all we knew, we were looking forward to the fight, and we didn't know how serious it was because we'd never been in war before. To us it was just one big adventure! And so marching through the town like that. The mayor even proclaimed a holiday! But we couldn't enjoy it, we were marched three miles out of town to do some training with the French, they were very co-operative, they gave us their artillery! Most of them were, sort of, short stature, and it seemed they had their clothes on for a year, but they were very nonchalant about everything. I guess they were very tired and pretty surprised to see that we were so eager to get into the fight.

NEWTON: Thank God you came.

TODD: We thought, 'Did you know what you were getting into?'

HAINES: Boy, we knew nothing. First thing we saw was these Frenchmen taking off their shirts in the evening, and

49

running the seams over the candle-flame, and there'd be this flick, flick, flick. They were cooking the coodies!

HARRIS: What?

HAINES: The coodies.

HARRIS: Coodies?

HAINES: Lice.

HARRIS: Lice! Hey, let me tell you about lice.

HAINES: The French were cooking them in the candles and they were going pop!

HARRIS: I went home for leave and ended up, stood outside my mother's house, taking them out of me armpits in handfuls.

HAINES: Well the French were cooking them! I mean I've heard of French cuisine!

HARRIS: She wouldn't let me in! Hadn't seen me for two years, wouldn't let me in!

HAINES: The next day we had hundreds and thousands of them ourselves and we went through the same pastime with the French in the coody situation.

HARRIS: The coody situation!

KITTY: (*A little flirty.*) Only thing to do was strip you.

HAINES: (*Grins.*) Yeah?

KITTY: When you got home. Of your uniform. And boil it in a copper.

HAINES: (*Flirty back.*) Oh, I see. What's your name?

KITTY: Kitty.

HAINES: Kitty.

NEWTON suddenly gets up.

NEWTON: I couldn't stand any more!

HAINES: Sorry? Sir?

NEWTON: For God's sake it had taken us three years to go eight miles, and now we were pulling back over the same ground. I'm sorry, I couldn't stand it!

HAINES: Sure, you guys. I mean you'd been there a long time.

TODD: You see, my friend, what was happening was, at this time, they were coming back off the Russian Front, like ghosts of the dead out of the East, hundreds of thousands of them. There wasn't anything we could do. Except pull back. Retreat again!

NEWTON picks up his notebook and puts it his bag.

NEWTON: It was hopeless. Absolutely hopeless. I put all the wounded into a cave, trying to keep them out of it, but the shelling got worse and...then the cave came down.

Pause.

They were buried alive.

Pause.

Captain Toye came round and said, 'You've got to get out of this as quick as you can, but you're going to have a hell of a walk.'

Desolate at the memory.

He meant because of the barrage. We walked through it all night. There were a hundred and eighty of us when we started and twenty-one when we arrived. I couldn't believe that such a thing could be happening. It was so like a nightmare that I thought it must actually be a nightmare. I had a sergeant walking beside me. Suddenly, a shell went up and as the smoke cleared I saw him sitting with his two stumps waving in the air, his legs completely shot off. I didn't know what to say. I said, 'Well, we'll take you to the side of the road.' He said, 'You're not going to leave me here?' I said, 'I'm afraid we can't do anything about it, we've got no stretcher-bearers, we've got nothing to carry you with, and we've got nothing to give you, but we'll put you out of the way of the tanks and I hope you'll be picked up.'

He stops, desperate.

That was a terrible decision. People who could walk helped the others along. I had about five people clinging to me, one with a jaw blown away, bleeding all over me, and that's how we ended our march. Getting through that was a miracle really, a miracle.

He stops, wants to say more, but can't.

I... I'm sorry. Very sorry.

He begins to go out, head bowed and upset, but is going in the wrong direction. HARRIS gently motions towards the door. NEWTON nods his gratitude, straightens, and leaves as an officer would. A silence, broken as usual by HARRIS.

HARRIS: Anyone ever heard of a place called Albert?

TODD: With the Madonna?

HARRIS: That's it. There was this legend that on the day this Madonna fell, the war would finish. So I said, 'Let's knock her down then and it'll finish now.' No one was listening.

HAINES: We were listening. That's why we came.

TODD turns to HAINES.

TODD: It was bad, you see? We were pulling back and I dropped down into this trench. I thought it looked familiar.

Can't believe it.

It was the one I'd been in two years before!

And then we moved back again, even further back. The French started throwing rocks at us and calling us cowards.

HARRIS: Remember Haig. General bloody Haig.

Imitates Haig.

'There is no other course open to us but to fight it out. Every position must be held to the last man. There can be no more retirement. We stand with our backs to the wall and believing in the justice of our cause each one of us must fight on to the end.'

Salutes sarcastically.

TODD: I couldn't have gone back anymore anyway. Didn't have the legs. This was it. They told us to rest. And wait.

Both HARRIS and TODD sit listlessly. HAINES is full of energy as he tells his story.

HAINES: We pushed forward. I mean, we got into the trucks and we moved up to the front, so then we could push forward. People came out and cheered us and you know, gave us their blessing.

KITTY is rapt. HARRIS and TODD sit silent, looking away.

When we got to the front I could see the Germans, they weren't more than a few hundred yards away. I could see their ambulances driving along the ridge to pick up their wounded. We worked hard to strengthen our position, because, at this point, so I'm told, we were the only defence between Paris and the enemy. That was a huge responsibility, but we knew there was going to be a big attack which would be the kind of fighting that we knew about. We didn't like trenches, no sir, we like open warfare. The way our ancestors had fought on the frontiers and in all the wars of our country. And that's what we wanted and that's what we looked forward to.

Getting excited.

So the big day came. It was a good sunny day.

TODD: That bloody day. It was raining.

HAINES: (*Quiet, enthralled.*) With just about five minutes before it was time to go over the top, everything was just as quiet as anything; you could hear a pin drop. And then, finally, five thousand guns started to fire over our heads and we jumped from our trenches and moved forward in line following the barrage. It was just like the fourth of July, there was so much noise going on. We were moving ahead with an unyielding determination to enforce our will on the enemy. When we got to the first trenches a lot of Germans were dead already from the artillery. We jumped over them and went on to the second line of trenches where there were some guys with their hands up. We could see

53

how bad it had been for them. We could see they didn't have any food. They were so hungry that they'd shot a horse and cut steaks out of the rump. And they hadn't even had time to bury their dead. But we didn't wait around. We travelled on through the wheat fields, the wheat was up to our hips, and we were under this terrific machine-gun fire. We ducked down and tried to go forward without being seen, but they fired their machine-guns through the wheat.

Pause.

You know when we started out we were five paces apart. Before long we were fifty yards apart, and then even as much as a hundred yards apart. I mean, that was the losses. The gaps in the line were so big that before long the captain is telling me to go and tell the fellers to close in to the right. So I started across the wheat, parallel with the front to do my mission.

Pause.

TODD: We went over for the last time. This had to be it, the last bloody time. In the end we were like a bunch of bloody madmen! We lost our senses. I lost mine anyhow. I exploded. I went absolutely crazy. That's because it had to be all over. I knew that. We couldn't stand any more. Nor could they. I don't remember much about it.

HARRIS: I've never seen so many tanks. It were easy, you just walked behind them as they went through the wire.

HAINES: And as I started out one German machine-gun in high ground there, had me spotted. He started to fire, and I could tell by the bark of the gun, when he had its muzzle trained on me. So I pretended that I got hit and went down. He turned his gun in another direction. I got up after about ten seconds or so and I continued another twenty, thirty yards. Then again he noticed that I wasn't really hit, that I was just fooling him and he turned his gun on me again, and again he fired. So I fooled him again. The third time I got close to where my buddy was, and I waved my arm to tell him to close in, and that same

German machine-gun that tried twice before to get me, saw me again, and finally got me.

KITTY: He got you?

HAINES: It wasn't too bad. I was OK.

HARRIS: We crossed over the fields. The Germans were pulling back. There were hundreds of planes in the sky.

TODD: I took a bayonet in the arm.

HAINES: I know the rest of my company went after them, never stopped, night after night, day after day.

HARRIS: And the Australians. I met a Canadian, he invited me to Ottawa.

TODD: Suddenly there were thousands of us.

HAINES: Moving forward. Together.

HARRIS: It got very quiet.

KITTY: You could smell it coming, couldn't you? We could, even at home.

HAINES: My Company captured their artillery: that was about two-and-a-half miles behind their lines.

HARRIS: They weren't bloody there any more.

HAINES: They were running back to Berlin!

TODD: Then there was this great shout!

HARRIS: It were bloody victory!

A pause. Lighter.

TODD: Someone told me there was this one group of Germans kept on firing until precisely eleven o'clock when the armistice was supposed to start. Then the officer stepped out of their position, stood up, lifted his helmet, bowed, and fell all his men in, in the open in front, and marched them off. Eleven o'clock. He trusted us, you see?

HARRIS: It were all over.

A pause.

HAINES: And we celebrated, boy did we celebrate!

HARRIS: We were in this estaminet and the owner gave us free drinks, then went to bed and left us to it.

HAINES: We drank to the men who weren't with us. We'd all come a long way. All of us.

HARRIS: Bloody long way.

HAINES: A long way. To them.

The others drink, or nod.

HARRIS / TODD / KITTY: To them.

A pause.

HAINES: Nice to meet you fellers.

TODD: Right.

KITTY: And you.

HAINES: Ma'am.

KITTY: Bye.

HAINES touches his hat and goes.

HARRIS: See yer, Yank.

KITTY: I heard it on the radio. People started going out onto the street. Nobody knew what to say. We just looked at each other.

HARRIS: A couple of blokes stole a jar of rum to celebrate. Next morning they were dead. They'd drank so much they'd choked it up and drowned themselves. Their faces were white as marble.

He pauses.

Everybody was there in the end. All the bloody dead an' all.

Sings.

'O for the wings of a dove.
Far, far away would I rove.'

He stops.

That's me. Nice to meet yer. Get me train now.

KITTY: Goodbye, love.

HARRIS: Bye.

Nods to TODD.

TODD: Bye, mate.

HARRIS goes.

KITTY: No one knew what we were going to do next. It was the end of a life. We'd all been young when it started.

TODD: I stood on a railway bank that the Manchesters had lined up on in 1914. At the bottom their skeletons were still there with their boots on, very still, no helmets, no rusty rifles or equipment, just their boots. And this cloud of white butterflies.

KITTY: It wasn't like London where they all got drunk of course. No, it wasn't like that, it was all very quiet. Well it was at first. It wasn't later.

TODD gets up and starts to pull his coat on.

TODD: I went down to the Sergeant's Mess. We had drinks and stood on chairs and tables and sang 'Auld Lang Syne'. After that everything went mad. They were throwing bombs into the sea for a laugh. But I knew that as soon it stopped that the old world would go. I was proud I had lived in it though. I missed it already. I missed the excitement. I missed the battlefields. There was no more moon rising over Dead Mule Corner, no more howitzers in their pits with their snouts up, and no fire coming from them. No more orders. No more Very lights, machine gun bullets. Nothing.

Pause.

And the men. No more men. I missed them most of all.

This upsets him.

I do now. I loved them to death.

Smiles.

Bye love. God Bless.

He goes. A silence. KITTY stands. She looks round at the empty space.

KITTY: I heard the postman come and knew it would be for me. I ran down in my nightdress, opened the door, snatched the letter off him and ran in and shut the door again.

She pauses.

I opened the letter and I saw it was from his sergeant. It just said, 'Dear Mrs Proctor, I'm very sorry to tell you of the death of your husband.' Well, that was as far as I could read. I don't really know what happened over the next few minutes, but I must have run out of the house as I was, in my bare feet, and banged on the next door. She let me in and said, 'Whatever's to do?' And I said, 'Would you read this letter, Mrs Hurst?' So she did, then said, 'Oh you poor child.' They brought some blankets and wrapped me up in them and sent word to my mother, so she came home and they treated me for shock.

Pause.

But his letter was only from his sergeant, and I thought perhaps it was a mistake. So I wrote back to him.

Pauses.

Then I got back another letter to say that this sergeant had also been killed. Later on, I got the official news.

Pauses.

It was all over.

All over for me then.

Peoperly all over.

She puts her coat on and slowly leaves the stage as the lights fade to blackout.

Ends.